Purchased With READ TO ACHIEVE Funds

Marine Life For Young Readers

MW00338572

Second Grade

Seals & Sea Lions

Contents

Text by Stanley L. Swartz
Photography by Robert Yin

DOMINIE PRESS
Pearson Learning Group

About Seals & Sea Lions

Seals and sea lions are close relatives. They are alike in many ways. Both are **mammals** that live on the land and in the water.

◄ Young Male Elephant Seal

Male seals and sea lions are called bulls. Females are called cows. Their babies are called pups. The pups are usually born on land.

◀ **Baby Harbor Seal**

Where They Live

Most seals and sea lions are found along the coast. They swim in **shallow** water. Their main enemies are sharks and killer whales.

◄ Harbor Seals near San Diego, California

How They Swim

Seals and sea lions have four **flippers**.
They have two flippers in front
and two in back. Seals and sea lions
are good swimmers.

◄ Group of Sea Lions under Water

Sea lions use their front flippers to swim quickly. They use their back flippers to **steer**. They use all four flippers to move on land.

◀ **Sea Lions Playing under Water**

Seals use their front flippers to steer in the water. They move their back flippers from side to side to swim. When they are on land, their **hind** flippers are useless.

◄ Harbor Seals on the Beach

What They Eat

Seals and sea lions have sensitive **whiskers** on their faces. Their whiskers help them search for food. Their favorite foods are fish, squid, octopus, and shellfish.

◀ Baby Harbor Seal

How They Stay Warm

Seals and sea lions have a thick layer of fat under their fur. This fat, or **blubber**, keeps them warm.

◀ Elephant Seals on the Beach

Their Ears

Sea lions have ear flaps. The male sea lion has a fury **mane** like a lion. They bark and grunt at each other. Sea lions have been taught to do tricks.

◀ Sea Lion under Water

Seals do not have **external** ear flaps. They have a small ear opening. This opening closes when they dive.

◀ Harbor Seal on the Beach

Caution! Wild Animals

These seals are sunning themselves on the **beach**. The people are walking very close to them. But they should be careful. Seals are **wild** animals!

◀ Harbor Seals and People Sharing the Beach

Glossary

beach:	The shore
blubber:	A thick layer of fat
external:	Outside
flippers:	Wide, flat body parts used for swimming
hind:	Back
mammals:	Warm-blooded animals
mane:	Long hair around an animal's neck
shallow:	Not deep
steer:	To guide
whiskers:	Long, stiff hairs
wild:	Animals that are not tame

Index